Colophon

©Mathias Jansson (2025)

" Black Metal in Contemporary Art: From Subcultural Darkness to the White Cube"

ISBN 978-91-86915-85-8

Published by:

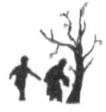 "jag behöver inget förlag"

c/o Mathias Jansson

Tvärvägen 23

232 52 Åkarp

SWEDEN

http://mathiasjansson72.blogspot.se/

Print: Lulu.com

Disclaimer: This book is written with help of ChatGPT. The author has previously conducted extensive research on the subject and has also contributed with texts about black metal and contemporary art in different journals. The text have been improved, edited and proofread by the author before publishing.

Content

Introduction 3
The history of Black Metal 5
The Darkness in Art History 11
When Black Metal and Art History Converge 16
Interviews and Texts about Artists Active in the Period Around 2010 21
Om ljuset tar oss: Exhibition 22
Nordic Darkness: Exhibition 26
Viktor Rosdahl: From *Panzerfaust* to Canvas 30
Haidar Mahdi: Black Metal and Ceramics 34
Johan Bergström: *Pagan Postcards* 38
Monica Winther and Kjersti Vetterstad: *Daughters of Valhalla* 42
Amelia Ishmael: Bringing Black Metal into Academia . 46
Bjarne Melgaard: Sons of Odins 52
Peter Beste and Torbjørn Rødland: Photography and Black Metal 55
Maddie Leach: *The Grief Prophesy* 57
Banks Violette: Black Metal Church 59
Élodie Lesourd: Deconstructing Black Metal 62
Summary 65

Introduction

There is a darkness that has always fascinated humanity. From the shadowed forests of Nordic landscapes to the candle-lit halls of Gothic cathedrals, artists have long been drawn to the mysterious, the uncanny, and the forbidden. Black metal, a music genre that erupted in the cold Norwegian winters of the 1980s and 1990s, channels this fascination with darkness in a way that is at once aggressive, poetic, and intensely visual. Its raw sound, icy melodies, and controversial mythology have captured the imagination of not only musicians but also visual artists around the world.

This book explores the meeting point of black metal and contemporary art—a place where music becomes image, sound becomes installation, and subculture becomes exhibition. While black metal began as a rebellious, underground movement, its influence has rippled far beyond the confines of record labels and concert halls. Artists have absorbed its aesthetics, themes, and rituals, translating them into painting, sculpture, installation, and even immersive sound experiences. Darkness, nature, myth, and ritual are no longer only heard—they are seen, felt, and entered.

You do not need to be a black metal fan to appreciate the art inspired by it. Whether it is the haunting landscapes of album covers, the immersive installations in a gallery, or the enigmatic figures captured in contemporary paintings, black metal has become a lens through which artists explore identity, alienation, mythology, and the human fascination with the unknown.

In these pages, you will discover the origins of black metal, its history, and its global cultural impact. You will meet the illustrators and artists who defined its visual language, explore international exhibitions that bring the music into the gallery, and encounter contemporary creators who continue to push the boundaries of sound, image, and ritual. Most of all, you will see how a genre often associated with rebellion and extremity has inspired a rich, multi-dimensional artistic conversation—a dialogue between music, visual culture, and the enduring human fascination with darkness.

Step into this world, where music and art collide, and discover how black metal's shadows illuminate the contemporary art scene in ways you may never have imagined.

The history of Black Metal

Black metal is more than a genre of music. It is a sound, an image, and a mythology that has haunted culture since its birth. To understand its power in contemporary art, we must first return to where it all began—in the shadows of the early 1980s, when a handful of bands lit the first flames of a new and terrifying movement.

The story often begins with Venom, a band from Newcastle, England. Their 1982 album *Black Metal* gave the genre its name. Venom's music was crude, fast, and chaotic, but it was their imagery that truly set them apart. Pentagrams, goat heads, leather, and spikes were splashed across their records and stages, creating a dark theater of the diabolical. They were not polished heavy metal like Iron Maiden, nor virtuosic like Judas Priest. Venom thrived in the raw, the aggressive, and the profane—a seed of rebellion.

At the same time, bands like Celtic Frost from Switzerland expanded the possibilities of extreme music. Their sound was heavy and strange, filled with doom-laden riffs, experimental touches, and lyrics about death, mythology, and cosmic horror. Bathory, from Sweden, brought another key element: an obsession with northern landscapes, pagan myths, and atmosphere. Bathory's early records laid the groundwork for what would become black metal's most defining features—cold guitar tones, shrieking vocals, and an almost ritualistic focus on darkness, death, and the old gods of Scandinavia.

Together, Venom, Celtic Frost, and Bathory formed what is often called the first wave of black metal. Their music and imagery were a blueprint: fast, raw, and anti-mainstream, wrapped in occult symbols and mythic darkness. Yet black metal, as we know it today, would only truly emerge in the early 1990s, in the icy landscapes of Norway.

True Norwegian Black Metal

This was the birth of True Norwegian Black Metal—a small, underground scene of young musicians who wanted to push extreme music further than anyone had dared before. Bands like Mayhem, Darkthrone, Emperor, Burzum, and Immortal took inspiration from their predecessors but stripped away the polish and theatrics. Instead, they embraced lo-fi recordings, harsh, freezing guitar tones, and shrieked vocals that sounded almost inhuman. Their music felt like a storm: cold, relentless, and uncompromising.

But black metal was never just about sound. It was also about ideas. The Norwegian scene drew inspiration from Satanism, paganism, and ancient Norse mythology, but also from philosophy, nihilism, and a rejection of modern society. They despised commercial culture and sought to create something pure, dangerous, and authentic. Darkness was not just an aesthetic—it was a worldview.

The scene became infamous for its extremity. In the early 1990s, church burnings across Norway shocked the world, and violent crimes associated with the movement gave black metal a reputation as the most dangerous music on earth. While the sensational headlines often overshadowed the music itself, they also made black metal into a cultural phenomenon—a symbol of rebellion, mystery, and forbidden knowledge.

Aesthetic of Black Metal

What makes black metal so enduring is that it is not only a genre of music but also a complete aesthetic system. It is about atmosphere as much as riffs, about imagery as much as sound. The corpse paint, the spidery band logos, the photographs taken in forests and ruins—these are as important as the songs themselves. Black metal created its own visual mythology, one that artists and audiences still recognize instantly: a world of frost, shadows, ritual, and resistance.

If black metal is a sound, it is also an image. From its earliest days, the genre built a visual identity that was as essential as the music itself. These images were not decorations—they were weapons, signals, and spells that told you exactly what world you were entering.

The most iconic of these images is corpse paint. Inspired partly by horror films, shock rockers like Alice Cooper, and the theatrics of bands such as Kiss, black metal musicians transformed it into something colder and more terrifying. Painted in black and white, faces became death masks, stripped of humanity, resembling the frozen expressions of the dead. For fans and artists alike, corpse paint was more than stage make-up—it was ritual armor, a way of erasing individuality and embodying the spirit of the music itself.

Lord of the Logos

Another crucial part of black metal's visual identity is its logos. Unlike the bold, simple logos of rock or punk, black metal bands embraced intricate, almost unreadable designs. They sprawled like tangled roots, cracked like frost across glass, or dripped like blood.

Belgian artist Christophe Szpajdel, often called the "Lord of the Logos," designed hundreds of these for underground bands as Emperor, Enthroned, Moonspell, and Old Man's Child. His work fused natural forms—branches, antlers, bones—with abstract geometry, creating symbols that looked both ancient and alien. These logos became talismans, visual mantras that marked belonging to the cult of black metal.

In 2011–2012, Christophe Szpajdel was invited by the Walker Art Center to create a special version of their logo, in conjunction with the exhibition *Graphic Design: Now in Production*.

Black metal logos are instantly recognizable for their ornate, organic lettering, drawing on Gothic architecture, Celtic ornamentation, and Jugendstil curves, often pushed to near-illegibility in a dense, baroque flourish. Szpajdel's Walker logo, while clearly inspired by this aesthetic, is surprisingly restrained, minimal compared with his usual work. The result is a striking hybrid: a major art institution borrowing the language of one of the most extreme subcultures in contemporary music, showing how underground visual forms can migrate into mainstream spaces while retaining their dark, intricate resonance.

Landscapes

The landscapes of black metal are another key element. Promotional photos were rarely taken in studios; instead, bands were photographed in forests, on snowy mountainsides, or before ruined churches. The natural world became a stage—cold, hostile, and eternal. These landscapes were not backgrounds but characters: symbols of isolation, rebellion against modern life, and a return to something raw and elemental.

Album covers also carried this atmosphere. Early black metal releases often featured stark black-and-white photography, runic symbols, or blurred, grainy images that enhanced their underground mystique. Later, illustrators and painters expanded this imagery into elaborate fantasy, mythology, and cosmic horror. These covers—whether minimal or maximal—served as gateways. Before the needle touched the record, the listener had already stepped into another world.

Taken together—corpse paint, logos, landscapes, album art—black metal created a total aesthetic environment. It was immersive, demanding, and instantly recognizable. It told stories without words, and it communicated values: rawness over polish, mystery over clarity, ritual over performance. This visual language not only gave black metal its identity but also laid the foundation for its influence on contemporary art.

The Darkness in Art History

"The oldest and strongest emotion of mankind is fear, and the oldest and strongest kind of fear is fear of the unknown."
— H. P. Lovecraft

Darkness is the realm of the unknown. It conceals what is hidden, what cannot be controlled, and what may never be understood. For centuries, artists have turned toward this obscurity, not away from it. To paint darkness, to sculpt death, to write of ruins and graveyards, is to grapple with the deepest emotions that bind humanity together: fear, awe, longing, and fascination with what lies beyond life.

Long before black metal's harsh guitars and shrieking voices carried these themes into music, art history was already steeped in shadow. Still lifes, Gothic cathedrals, Romantic landscapes, and the grotesque visions of Goya all remind us that the fascination with death and the "other side" has always been part of culture. Black metal simply inherited—and amplified—a tradition centuries in the making.

Vanitas and the Still Life of Death

In the Dutch and Flemish Golden Age, artists transformed the humble still life into a meditation on existence itself. Painters such as Pieter Claesz, Harmen Steenwijck, and Willem Claeszoon Heda became masters of the vanitas tradition. On their canvases, glimmering goblets, half-peeled lemons, fine silver, and books of learning stand alongside skulls, broken glass, extinguished candles, and rotting fruit.

The message was clear: beauty fades, knowledge crumbles, wealth cannot save you. Everything is vanity; everything is fleeting. These canvases whispered *memento mori*—remember that you will die.

Others carried the genre into darker territory. *Philippe de Champaigne's Vanitas Still Life* (1671), with its stark skull, tulip, and hourglass, strips away the richness of detail to show death, life, and time in stark balance. The painting resembles a visual manifesto for black metal's obsession with mortality: austere, minimal, uncompromising.

Where popular culture today hides decay, these artists insisted on showing it—just as black metal insists on screaming it.

The Gothic Imagination

The Gothic style was born in the 12th century with its soaring cathedrals and grotesque gargoyles. Yet its legacy lingered into the modern era, becoming a wellspring for artists fascinated by ruin and shadow.

When the Gothic Revival swept Europe in the 18th and 19th centuries, ruins became central motifs. Hubert Robert, known as "Robert of the Ruins," painted grandiose images of crumbling abbeys and collapsed temples, often populated by tiny human figures dwarfed by stone and shadow. His works suggested both nostalgia and awe at the destructive power of time.

In England, John Constable and J.M.W. Turner also turned their gaze toward ruined castles and storm-swept landscapes. Constable's melancholic views of Stonehenge or Turner's turbulent skies over Gothic spires captured a tension between nature, faith, and human fragility.

Romanticism and the Sublime

If Gothic ruins evoked melancholy, the Romantic movement elevated darkness into something vast and overwhelming: the sublime.

The German painter Caspar David Friedrich is perhaps the most emblematic. His *Abbey in the Oakwood* (1809–10) shows monks carrying a coffin through a barren grove toward a ruined church. The skeletal trees, foggy twilight, and broken architecture combine into a vision of both mourning and transcendence. In *The Sea of Ice* (1823–24), jagged shards of frozen sea engulf a shipwreck—a symbol of humanity crushed by nature's indifference.

Elsewhere, painters like John Martin in England filled massive canvases with apocalyptic visions: collapsing cities, floods, infernos. Works such as *The Great Day of His Wrath* (1851–53) turned biblical destruction into sublime spectacle.

These Romantic works echo black metal's own landscapes: vast, unforgiving, annihilating. Both turn forests, mountains, and storms into symbols of eternity, dwarfing the human presence.

The Terrible Beauty of Goya

Where Friedrich sought solemn transcendence, Francisco de Goya plunged headlong into nightmare. His *Disasters of War* series (1810–20) exposed human cruelty in stark etchings of mutilation and death. But it was his late *Black Paintings* (1819–23) that fully revealed his vision of darkness.

On the walls of his home, Goya painted twisted figures, witches' sabbaths, and grotesque demons. The most infamous, *Saturn Devouring His Son*, shows the Titan devouring the body of his child, eyes wide with horror. Another, *Witches' Sabbath*, depicts a goat-headed figure presiding over a circle of terrified women.

These paintings anticipate modern horror imagery, combining the grotesque, the sacrilegious, and the uncanny. In their raw, unflinching portrayal of despair, they share a kinship with black metal's own refusal to look away from darkness.

Forests and Graveyards

The forest has always been a place of mystery, fear, and imagination. In folklore and Romantic art alike, it was a site of both danger and transcendence: where spirits lurked, where wanderers vanished, where the sacred and the uncanny converged. Painters like Friedrich returned again and again to the motif of the dark forest as a space of solitude, death, and revelation.

Graveyards, too, captured the imagination. The churchyard scenes painted by Friedrich, or the melancholy cemetery etchings by artists such as Giovanni Battista Piranesi, made tombs and monuments into landscapes of reflection. In Piranesi's *Imaginary Prisons* series, although not literal graveyards, the monumental arches and endless stairways evoke the same suffocating sense of death's architecture.

Black metal would later reclaim these spaces as its natural stage: band photos shot among tombstones, lyrics invoking the silence of the forest, album covers adorned with ruins and graveyards. These places remain powerful because they are thresholds—the meeting ground of life and death, the known and the unknown.

When Black Metal and Art History Converge

From its earliest days, black metal has carried within it a powerful visual and symbolic dimension, drawing heavily on the history of art to give shape to its own dark universe. The black-and-white aesthetic of early Norwegian demo tapes already suggested a fascination with atmosphere and imagery, but as the genre matured, it began to interact more explicitly with both historical painting and the contemporary art world.

Satyricon and the Munch Museum

One of the most striking examples of this dialogue came in 2022, when the band Satyricon collaborated with the Munch Museum in Oslo. Instead of treating music as an accompaniment, the project presented sound and painting as equal partners, with Satyricon composing an entire work to be experienced alongside Edvard Munch's brooding images. The exhibition became a meeting point between two kinds of Norwegian darkness: the existential anxieties of Munch's brushstrokes and the bleak intensity of black metal soundscapes. It was a reminder that the genre, often dismissed as underground rebellion, has found resonance within the very institutions of cultural heritage.

Romanticism and Symbolism in Black Metal Imagery

Black metal's relationship to art history runs deeper than these contemporary collaborations. The genre has long turned to the Romantic and Symbolist traditions of the nineteenth century for its imagery. Theodor Kittelsen's illustrations, with their spectral forests, folkloric creatures, and allegories of death, have become almost synonymous with the Norwegian black metal aesthetic. His drawing *Op under Fjeldet toner en Lur* graces the cover of Burzum's *Filosofem*, and in doing so, it bridges a century of cultural history. What was once an expression of national romanticism in art became, in the hands of Varg Vikernes, an emblem of black metal's immersion in both nature and myth.

The Romantic painters more broadly—Caspar David Friedrich in Germany, Johan Christian Dahl and Marcus Larson in Scandinavia—offered landscapes that continue to echo in the visual world of the genre. Their canvases, with fog-draped mountains, solitary figures dwarfed by storms, and forests heavy with melancholy, carry the same emotional weight that black metal strives for in sound. This connection was made explicit in the exhibition *Skräckromantikens landskap* at the Gothenburg Museum of Art in 2014–2015, which placed nineteenth-century Romantic paintings in conversation with the Gothic and metal subcultures of today. Visitors moving from the sublime drama of Larson's storm paintings to contemporary goth aesthetics could trace a continuous fascination with the beauty and terror of darkness.

Album Covers as Modern Iconography

Album covers have perhaps been the most immediate bridge between black metal and visual art. The Swedish painter Kristian "Necrolord" Wåhlin has become legendary for his work with bands like Emperor, Dissection, and Dark Funeral, creating oil-on-canvas visions of ruined cathedrals, twilight landscapes, and spectral figures. His paintings carry the weight of Caspar David Friedrich and Hieronymus Bosch, yet are inseparable from the music they represent.

In Poland, the apocalyptic surrealism of Zdzisław Beksiński has likewise found its way into black and extreme metal covers, his nightmare architectures becoming a visual equivalent of black metal's sound. In more recent years, artists such as Zbigniew M. Bielak have continued this tradition, producing elaborate illustrations for bands like Watain that draw on Gothic, Romantic, and occult imagery with painstaking detail.

Gaahl as Painter

What makes black metal distinctive, however, is that the visual realm is not outsourced but often arises from within the scene itself. Many musicians are also practicing visual artists.

Kristian "Gaahl" Espedal, long known for his role in Gorgoroth, has in recent years become equally recognized as a painter. His art is marked by solitary figures, muted colours, and a meditative intensity that reflects inner states rather than outward appearances. Often working in cold tones and stark contrasts, Gaahl seeks to reveal what he calls the "ghosts within" — memories, unseen forces, and layers of identity.

There is a clear resonance with Edvard Munch. Like Munch, Gaahl uses the human figure not as portraiture but as a vessel for emotion and existential solitude. Where Munch dissolved his subjects into restless brushstrokes, Gaahl reduces his palette, letting shadow and isolation dominate, but both artists aim to expose psychological truth over realism.

Gaahl also runs Galleri Fjalar in Bergen, where his works stand in dialogue with other artists. In these settings, Gaahl emerges not only as a musician but as a visual artist continuing a Nordic lineage of painting the unseen — from Munch's anguished figures to his own spectral, introspective visions.

Other Black Metal Artists as Painters

Besides Gaahl, there are several notable black metal musicians whose visual art is integral to their creative identity. Sindre Foss Skancke, for example, whose project Utarm mixes black metal and funeral doom, has painted iconic covers like Dødsengel's *Mirium Occultum* (2010) and designed layout and logos for newer bands like RUÏM. His work has been shown widely across Norway, and internationally in Italy, France, Luxembourg, Germany, and Australia.

Erik Danielsson of Watain, under the name Trident Arts, produces visual work using collage, xerox, and halftone patterns, evoking a raw, abrasive energy. Vrangsinn and Nattefrost from Carpathian Forest engage deeply with painting and graphic art, often experimenting with unconventional materials such as blood, coal, and ashes. Kim Carlsson (ex-Lifelover) has likewise created disturbing artworks with visceral materials like blood, ashes, and milk, while Valnoir (Jean-Emmanuel Simoulin) of Metastazis blends graphic design with macabre experiments using bone-based inks and ritualistic imagery.

A Shared Lineage of Darkness

Together, these examples reveal that black metal is deeply entangled with art history. Its imagery is not accidental, nor is it a mere marketing tool, but part of a long cultural lineage of exploring darkness, nature, myth, and the sublime. From Kittelsen's forests to Munch's existential figures, from nineteenth-century Romantic landscapes to twenty-first-century museum collaborations, black metal situates itself as heir to a visual and intellectual tradition of melancholy and dread. It is a genre where the music cannot be separated from its imagery, because both are expressions of the same artistic obsession: to stare into the abyss, and to give it form.

Interviews and Texts about Artists Active in the Period Around 2010

Om ljuset tar oss: Exhibition

In June 2011, Gävle Art Center presented the exhibition *Om ljuset tar oss* ("If the Light Takes Us"), featuring works by artists as Monica Winther, Kjersti Vetterstad, Petr Davydtchenko, and Viktor Rosdahl. The works relate in various ways to black metal, especially the second wave that emerged in Norway in the late 1980s and early 1990s with bands like Burzum, Darkthrone, Emperor, Immortal, and Mayhem.

Interview from 2011 with curators: Carl Bergström, Joakim Forsgren and Maja-Lena Johansson.

Can you tell us how the idea for the exhibition came about? Why black metal specifically? And how are you collaborating with Getaway Rock Festival this summer?

Carl Bergström: Joakim Forsgren, who is an artist and has exhibited at Gävle Art Center before, and I were talking about black metal, and the idea immediately arose to do an exhibition with contemporary artists whose work is in some way rooted in extreme metal. Gävle Art Center is housed in Silvanum, a building that was previously a forestry museum, creating a strong symbolic link to black metal, where forests play an important role and often appear in band photos, album covers, and music videos. At first, we considered a broader exhibition on forest and darkness, but over time we decided to focus entirely on artists with close ties to the black metal scene.

Joakim initially suggested organizing a performance by a prominent band in the genre in the forest visible from the Center's panoramic windows. When we realized the exhibition coincided with Getaway Rock Festival, a collaboration naturally made sense.

The Center seeks collaborations to gain expertise and partial funding. The festival happens every July, has significant reach locally and regionally, and gives us an opportunity to engage with a larger audience. By linking the exhibition to the festival, we hope to attract both contemporary art audiences and festival-goers. Admission is free, and while we don't rely on visitor numbers financially, our goal is to reach new audiences.

The exhibition is intended to function on two levels: first, to attract hard rock and metal fans who might not usually visit contemporary art exhibitions, and second, to introduce black metal as a cultural phenomenon to contemporary art audiences and other visitors.

You've created a Spotify playlist with selected black metal music for the exhibition. What are your own experiences and interests in black metal?
Carl Bergström: I listened to many of the first-wave black metal bands in the 1980s. When Swedish death metal began to grow in the late '80s, it and other extreme metal became my music. I drifted away when Swedish death metal became commercially successful around '91–'92. This commercialization was partly what the second wave of Norwegian black

metal reacted against. I stopped listening to metal for a time, though I followed the aesthetics of black metal in the early '90s—album art, design, imagery—without listening to the music. A few years ago, I revisited black metal and realized I had missed something; much of the music is fantastic.

Joakim Forsgren: I don't have a direct relationship to the black metal scene, but I'm interested in the intersection of music and art. I am both an artist and a bassist in the rock band The Scrags.

Maja-Lena Johansson: I listened to a lot of Swedish death metal in the early '90s, and many bands were inspired by black metal—stage shows, lyrics, films, and other elements. The aesthetics were fascinating, and I documented many concerts. It's very interesting to return to this world of symbols, narratives, and aesthetics twenty years later. Highlighting this genre in contemporary art, using music to illuminate the works, allows us to explore contemporary cultural history.

The exhibition takes its name from a Burzum album, and Varg Vikernes personally approved the use of his music in a video. How do you handle the fact that Vikernes is a controversial figure, convicted of murder and church arson?

Carl Bergström: *Om ljuset tar oss* is not a "black metal exhibition" in a narrow sense; it's an exhibition of four contemporary artists using black metal in different ways. We provide informational materials on-site that explain these nuances. For example, the text on Petr

Davydtchenko addresses these complexities. Trained staff are always available to guide visitors and answer questions.

Joakim Forsgren: Black metal explores humanity's dark side, approaching primal forces hidden beneath our social facades. The internal mythology and focus on Norse heritage are of interest to me. Bands like Ultima Thule and Burzum offer distorted versions of Norse mythology—Ultima Thule emphasizes heroic struggle, while Burzum focuses on dark primal forces. The music and aesthetics are of a high standard and appeal socially because of their intensity. The exhibition's title, *Om ljuset tar oss*, reflects a certain self-awareness: how do we relate to our dark sides?

I think that question unites the artists in this exhibition. Black metal is very physical—self-sacrifice and ecstatic intensity are central. Everything is pushed to the extreme: music, clothing, performance. Irony and self-distance rarely exist.

Why are so many contemporary artists interested in black metal today?
Joakim Forsgren: Norway's black metal wave can be seen as a response to cultural hypocrisy. Contemporary artists' interest may be a reaction to an art world overly focused on intellectual internalism. The artists in our exhibition engage physically with black metal, not distantly. They collide with the genre to see what new insights emerge about themselves and our contemporary world.

Nordic Darkness: Exhibition

Johan Zetterquist and Staffan Boije af Gennäs are Swedish curators known for their work in contemporary art exhibitions that explore darker themes in Nordic culture. In the exhibition *Nordic Darkness*, at Kristinehamn Art Museum 2011 they examined the darker sides of contemporary art, including references to the black metal music scene. The exhibition highlights how themes of darkness, chaos, and existential struggle have long inspired Nordic artists, and how black metal has become a visual and conceptual touchstone for contemporary artistic expression.

Interview from 2011 Johan Zetterquist and Staffan Boije af Gennäs on *Nordic Darkness*

"Nordic Darkness" focuses on the dark side of contemporary art, with many references to the black metal scene. How do you think black metal has inspired or influenced Nordic contemporary art?
Zetterquist: Visually, black metal has inspired many artists. It's a very visual phenomenon. Some of the artists in *Nordic Darkness*, like Roger and Daniel Andersson and Banks Violette, have a direct relationship to black metal, each approaching it in their own way. Fascination with black metal often becomes fascination with evil. Especially the Andersson brothers' works feel like a study of evil.

Cultural phenomena rarely appear in isolation. That black metal emerged at the same time as many artists—who had no prior connection to the music—were exploring dark themes in their work is not a coincidence. Black metal is the clearest expression of "contemporary darkness." When we began developing the exhibition, it became a natural reference.

There's something immediate in black metal's expression, in the experience of the music, something musical that translates into a tangible physical sensation. The aesthetic impact is contagious. Translating that into a visual form is very compelling.

Banks Violette (USA) has the most direct link to the Nordic black metal scene among the participating artists. If you want a visual connection to the music, you'll find it in his work.

What is your own relationship to black metal?
Zetterquist: I have a fairly intense relationship with black metal. I listen mostly to older material, which I find the most vital and musically interesting: Darkthrone, early Burzum, early Mayhem, and I love Striborg.

Boije af Gennäs: I don't listen to music very often in general. But I find black metal as a phenomenon very interesting. My fascination has led me to attend a few concerts and try to understand the music.

Could one say the exhibition reflects broader societal changes? The exhibition also includes

older works by Swedish artists as August Strindberg and Carl Fredrik Hill. Hasn't darkness always fascinated artists?
Darkness is by no means new—neither financial crises, environmental threats, racism, nor personal existential darkness. The exhibition includes many kinds of darkness. Matias Faldbakken and Gardar Einarsson's *Heroin Sofa*, Niklas Eneblom's *Pundare in a 242 on a roadside parking lot* reflect societal darkness, while Christine Ödlund's and C. F. Hill's drawings reflect personal darkness.
The idea for the exhibition came from observing trends in art, especially in Sweden, Norway, and Finland. We included Strindberg, Hill, Roy Friberg, and Theodor Kittelsen partly because they visually fit into contemporary art and partly to show that this "darkness" is not new but recurrent.

There may be societal changes behind the shift toward darker tones, but it's difficult to pinpoint exact causes. What is clear is that these changes have resulted in a lot of remarkable art.

In the catalog, you mention it was difficult to find suitable Danish artists for the exhibition. Why do you think that is?
Boije af Gennäs: We searched but only found a few works from Denmark that were relevant to the exhibition. The marked difference in the availability of dark-themed art compared to Sweden, Norway, and Finland was unexpected. I assume Denmark lacks the

same historical tradition. The preferred artistic motifs in Denmark are gray November weather; the winter night is more gray than pitch-black. There's no forest to hide in or mountains to jump from if life feels overwhelming.

According to international surveys, Danes are consistently ranked the happiest people in the world. While that designation may be simplistic, it says something about the culture. If you're looking for melancholy, you probably need to look elsewhere. The smaller black metal scene in Denmark compared to Sweden, Norway, and Finland may be related to this cultural "grayscale" in art.

How has the exhibition been received so far?
Boije af Gennäs: There are many excellent works in the exhibition. Locally in Kristinehamn, some were perhaps initially reserved about the exhibition, but after seeing it, their reservations disappeared. The question is how many people we've met in Stockholm, Gothenburg, and Copenhagen who said they would travel to Kristinehamn actually make the trip. It's a reasonably long journey. The "geographical resistance" has its own charm—people talk about the exhibition, but few come to see it. It's also fitting that the exhibition is at a museum in the woods. Many participating artists appreciated the location. Darkness should never be too crowd-pleasing; it needs a certain resistance.

Viktor Rosdahl: From *Panzerfaust* to Canvas

Viktor Rosdahl (b. 1973) is a Swedish contemporary visual artist whose work spans painting, installation, and mixed media. Drawing on music, literature, and subcultural aesthetics, Rosdahl explores themes of alienation, violence, and societal tension. His pieces have been exhibited at venues including Gävle Konstcentrum, where he participated in the exhibition Om ljuset tar oss.

Some works of culture strike you so deeply that they remain a lifelong companion. For Rosdahl, that work is Darkthrone's 1996 album Panzerfaust. The deliberately lo-fi sound, distant vocals, and visceral intensity of tracks like "Hans siste vinter," "En vind av sorg," and "The Hordes of Nebulah" left a lasting impression.

In this interview from 2011, Viktor Rosdahl discusses his relationship with black metal and how it inspires his art.

When did you start listening to black metal?
I gradually began listening to the music in the early 1990s. My older brothers, Ola and Anders, and I had been listening to hard rock since childhood—I bought my first record in 1986, *Twisted Sister*—and followed the genre's development through thrash and later releases from the label Earache. I also explored the death metal scene, with bands like Morbid Angel, Slayer, Cathedral, Entombed, Dismember, and later In

Flames' first two albums. From there, the step to Darkthrone, Emperor, Dissection, and side projects like Isengard and Mortiis wasn't far. At the same time, we ordered many releases from Cold Meat Industry, discovering the dark industrial ambient genre, and later bands within Neofolk, such as *The Moon Lay Hidden Beneath a Cloud*.

My brother and I also had our own black metal band, Riothamus, with a few others from Helsingborg. We were heavily inspired by Ved Buens Ende and their expressionist and psychedelic elements.

Is there a particular band or album that has meant more to you?
I'd say some of these bands and albums have stayed with me throughout my life, especially Darkthrone's *Panzerfaust*. The deliberately rough, cassette-like sound, the vocals sometimes seeming distant, and the music that hits you "right in the stomach" as people say—these have had a strong impact. On *Panzerfaust*, the tracks most important to me are "Hans siste vinter," "En vind av sorg," and "The Hordes of Nebulah," which features a guest appearance by Varg Vikernes.

How has black metal influenced you as an artist?
This entire genre has been, and continues to be, very significant for me. It has affected my life deeply, and I've found much joy in both the music and the anti-establishment themes. The vague sense of resistance to society, expressed in the lyrics and the overall

aesthetic, resonates with me. Many of my artworks include direct references or quotations from the black metal scene, though these often went unnoticed until Carl Bergström from Gävle Konstcentrum contacted me about a year and a half ago to collaborate on the exhibition *Om ljuset tar oss*.

Can you tell us about a work of yours inspired by black metal?
One of the most important pieces for me was created on a leather jacket, depicting a scene drawn from my own life—two youths fighting each other with axes. In this case, I adapted a scene from Jan Troell's film adaptation of *The Emigrants*. The leather jacket, with its cathedral-like arches, was then hung from a metal frame, similar to the "hangman" drawing game. For me, it explored what can happen when people are exposed to violence, how it can propagate through human relationships, and what it means to live as "condemned" in a society where violence is taboo, as well as living with strong hatred—sampled through the worlds of black metal and proletarian literature.

There are many preconceptions about black metal. This came up in debates around *Om ljuset tar oss* at Gävle Konstcentrum. How do you view this?
I understand that it can seem problematic to listen to music created by people with suspicious or, in some cases, outright foolish ideas and statements. I don't think it can be explained away with a simple "but." Perhaps these feelings of hatred and misanthropy are

always present in some individuals, regardless of society, and they cannot always be eliminated. The idea of pure, morally, humanistically instructive art and cultural expression is itself deeply repulsive in its didactic spirit. It's also worth noting that things are not always as black-and-white as they are sometimes described by outsiders with particular agendas using a subculture to push a certain narrative.

Haidar Mahdi: Black Metal and Ceramics

Haidar Mahdi (b. 1992) is a contemporary Swedish artist working primarily in ceramics. His practice explores the boundaries between traditional craft and contemporary subcultures, blending meticulous technique with provocative themes. Mahdi's master's exhibition at the Royal Institute of Art in Stockholm, *Black Mass (2011)*, investigated how the visual and conceptual language of black metal could be translated into ceramic forms such as candelabras and cake stands.

In this interview from 2011, Mahdi discusses his fascination with black metal and how it informs his artistic approach.

Can you tell us what was the starting point for your exhibition *Black Mass* and what about the black metal genre interested you?
For me, it felt quite natural for Black Metal to become a theme in my work. Hard rock has been my biggest interest since seventh grade, and I am surprised that it took me nearly 25 years to bring my greatest passion—music, alongside my artistic practice—into my work. It should have been obvious a long time ago. I have a deep knowledge of the culture after years of dedication, and when I see it as a source for my art, I see many interesting aspects and entry points. I think of all the details, such as studs, or how black is a recurring color in everything from clothing to hair.

I primarily work with clay, so the intersection of ceramics and Black Metal is what interests me most. In the contrast between soft and hard—where clay and ceramics represent softness and Black Metal hardness—a contradictory combination arises that is extremely exciting. Clay can be perceived as a conventional and traditional material. If one sees it that way, the distance to Black Metal feels very large.

Clay is often associated with something mossy or silly, or it is romanticized as something given to us by Mother Earth, or it is entirely associated with evening classes and coffee breaks. In my experience, clay has relatively low status in art circles, and for many it is considered quite uninteresting. Ceramic is ceramic. Period. I enjoy working in a material strongly associated with things outside the art world. But just because I enjoy that does not mean I want to work outside the art world.

What is your own relationship to black metal?
When I listen to the music, I feel evil and hatred, but above all seriousness. When these bands perform, it is not uncommon to see pig's blood and cadavers on stage. Their brutal and harsh way of spreading Satan's word fascinates me, and I wanted to use the feeling Black Metal evokes in my exhibition. A defining feature of Black Metal is the exaltation of evil and endurance of pain. Specifically, it is about not embracing what is natural (the good). If you embrace what is not natural, you embrace what is not good. They show this clearly

35

with their long hair, black clothing, studs, leather, pentagrams, and inverted crosses. There is also an emphasis on masculine aggression, which I partly want to embrace. But since I try to make something that I consider beautiful and work with my hands in a soft, organic material like clay, I simultaneously introduce a human touch. This creates a strong paradox in relation to Black Metal as a genre and lifestyle. In a way, I may be ridiculing everything they stand for, but at the same time, it is precisely what they stand for that I am working with. For me, this tension is irresolvable and something I believe is visible in my work.

Do you see any visual similarity between your ceramic works and the visual world of Black Metal? I do think there is a visual similarity between my ceramics and Black Metal, absolutely. Even though clay and ceramics are not the first thing that comes to mind when you hear or see Black Metal, I see my meticulous attention to detail and the gothic, ancient, almost Greek-white "marble-like" quality of my sculptures as a good reference. Some Black Metal bands are fascinated with Norse mythology, runes, and so on. The technical knowledge required for clay to make my exhibition possible is comparable to the attention to detail in the music and the entire genre. An inexperienced listener might claim that the fast "noise" and the "beast" or human behind the vocals is just rubbish. But here I perceive extreme instrumental skill, incredible detail, and excellent atmosphere creation.

How have you tried to visualize the genre in your work?
I have done my utmost to emulate and visualize the genre. I have tried to take everything into account—from the decadent lifestyle to album covers, to the myth of Black Metal as the devil-worshipping genre where murders and church burnings occur in Satan's name. In a constantly changing world, where people change with the wind, where words often amount to nothing but empty talk or status—as in living in a city like Stockholm—it feels incredibly satisfying to present Black Metal as something real. It is not just empty talk or rumors; this genre exists and acts in reality, for its beliefs. There are real people who love something, and that is something I hold in high regard. Therefore, with the greatest respect for all fans and bands, I have wanted to make my own interpretation of Black Metal in my own way.

Johan Bergström: *Pagan Postcards*

Johan Bergström (b.1978) is a Swedish photographer whose work explores the intersection of landscape, culture, and mythology. In his project, *Pagan Postcards*, examines the visual and symbolic relationship between Norwegian black metal and the wild, rugged landscapes of Norway. Through his lens, Bergström investigates how the imagery of black metal—steep mountains, dense forests, and icy fjords—reflects both fascination and fear of nature, drawing subtle connections to Romantic art and Nordic heritage.

Interview from 2011 with Johan Bergström.

Where does your interest in black metal come from, and how has the genre inspired your artistic practice?
I wouldn't say I have had a close relationship with the black metal scene, but I have followed it over the years through literature, interviews, documentaries, and occasional listening. There are so many interesting threads in black metal that have drawn me back to it: the attraction of darkness, criticism of civilization, sentimentality, and the tension between theatrical elements and the need for authenticity. Moreover, the music is so powerful that it is hard to resist. The fact that Norway became the platform for the second wave of black metal, and the genre's close relationship with nature, eventually became the starting point for *Pagan Postcards*. Inevitably, I view the scene from the

outside, and that is something I do not hide but rather try to make visible in my work. I haven't previously integrated black metal into my art, but looking back, most of my work contains dark threads expressed in different ways.

In your photographs, you've inserted quotes from various songs. How did you choose them? My focus was on Norwegian bands from the second wave of black metal. To set boundaries for myself, I read lyrics from around a hundred albums released by the most prominent Norwegian bands of the 1990s. I found it most relevant to work from the bands that established and defined the expression of the new wave. Some of the bands I referenced include Mayhem, Darkthrone, Burzum, Immortal, Emperor, Enslaved, Satyricon, Thorns, and Ulver—about twenty bands in total. From this material, I selected short text fragments addressing nature, the path toward darkness, and sentimentality. The lyrics I use should not be seen as the essence of the genre's message. I deliberately chose texts that, taken out of context, could be interpreted in multiple ways.

In your images, there is an unsettling contrast between the majestic, beautiful landscapes and quotes like "This is war" and "The water is my blood." It seems nature for many black metal bands symbolizes chaos, darkness, and war rather than the peaceful contemplation that Romanticism

sought. **Do you see other connections between Romantic ideals and Black Metal?**
Absolutely. Perhaps not in Norwegian Romantic landscape painting specifically, but in the broader ideas of Romanticism, I see intersections with black metal in terms of criticism of civilization, idealization of the past, striving for individuality, and the celebration of heroes or the "noble savage." Romanticism also placed great interest in folklore, mysticism, spirituality, occult rituals, and the study of evil. In both cases, nature stands as a symbol of the untamed or the past—a counterpoint to the modern, civilized, superficial, and materialistic world. I doubt they share the same utopia, but I simply wanted to see what would emerge from bringing them together. Before traveling to Norway to collect material, I drew inspiration from Romantic painting, including Norwegian artists Johan Christian Dahl, Hans Gude, and August Cappelen.

Can you tell us where the photographs were taken? Do the locations have any special connection to black metal?
The photographs were broadly taken within the Oslo, Bergen, and Trondheim regions, framing the Norwegian landscape as a whole. The exact location wasn't important beyond being Norwegian terrain. Anyone looking for black metal trivia in my landscapes will have to look hard. My ambition was to depict Norwegian nature in all the forms addressed in black

metal lyrics, from fjords to high mountains. This was accomplished over two solo road trips, which could be described as a sort of dérive through Norwegian wilderness with black metal as the soundtrack.

Monica Winther and Kjersti Vetterstad: *Daughters of Valhalla*

Monica Winther (b. 1976) and Kjersti Vetterstad (b. 1977) are Norwegian contemporary artists whose collaborative work explores the intersections of mythology, music, and visual culture. Their project, *Daughters of Valhalla*, was featured in the exhibition *Om ljuset tar oss* at Gävle Konstcentrum. The project investigates the influence of black metal and Norse mythology on contemporary art, blending ancient narratives with modern media to explore identity, cultural memory, and the tension between tradition and globalization.

Interview from 2011 with Monica Winther and Kjersti Vetterstad:

What is the work *Daughters of Valhalla* about?
The starting point for the exhibition in Gävle was the curators Carl Bergström, Maja-Lena Johansson, and assistant curator Joakim Forsgräns' interest in black metal and art influenced by Norway's second wave of black metal in the early 1990s. We were invited to participate with the video *The Giants of Yore*, which, as its presentation suggests, is part of a larger, ongoing project titled *Daughters of Valhalla*. The project is based on *Völuspá* (The Prophecy of the Völva), the first poem of the *Poetic Edda*.

In Norse mythology, a völva was a seeress who practiced prophecy and magic. In *Völuspá*, a völva tells Odin about the creation of the world, predicts the death of the god Balder, and foretells Ragnarok, the end of humans and gods. In the video *The Giants of Yore*, two jötnar (giants) wander through a snowy, picturesque landscape. They stop occasionally to eat, drink, and fight. Jötnar were enormous beings who lived in Útgard, the outermost of the three worlds under the ever-living tree Yggdrasil. *The Giants of Yore* are already mentioned in the second verse of *Völuspá*, when the völva recalls the creation of the world. This video is the first in a planned series that explores various figures and events from *Völuspá*, merging elements of Norse mythology with contemporary perspectives.

The music accompanying the video is taken from Burzum's album *Dauði Baldrs* (Balder's Death). The compositions used are "Í Heimr Heljar" and "Bálferð Baldrs." Burzum's musical interpretations of Norse myth, combined with his innovative sound, made his music meaningful for the project. Varg Vikernes—the man behind Burzum—shared the artist Theodor Kittelsen's (1857–1914) fascination with Norwegian culture, history, and nature, using several of Kittelsen's motifs for his album covers. For example, the cover of *Hvis Lyset Tar Oss* (1994) draws from Kittelsen's depictions of the Black Death in Norway. The video was filmed in Sigdal, near Laulia, where Kittelsen spent ten of his most productive years as a landscape painter and illustrator of Norwegian folklore.

In the exhibition *Om ljuset tar oss*, we also presented *Heimdall – Valhalla Border Surveillance*, a six-meter-high border watchtower, and *The Arrival of Fenrir*, a postcard depicting a figure with black hair, dressed in wolfskin, crouching in a desolate black stone landscape while playing a bone flute. Both works are part of the *Daughters of Valhalla* project, developed during the planning of the Gävle exhibition.

Daughters of Valhalla can be understood as a free improvisation on the *Edda* poem, interpreting the völva's prophecy and her role as a storyteller and seer within a contemporary context. The works reflect humanity's search for identity through cultural and mythical roots in a media-synchronized, market-driven, and globalized world, questioning the commercial forces shaping national identity and the exoticization of culture and nature that results.

What significance has black metal had for your artistic practice?
Although we both have an affinity for black metal, the genre does not hold a significant place in our artistic practice outside this specific project. In the video *The Giants of Yore*, the use of Burzum's music and black metal's aesthetic codes functions as a conceptual device. That said, 1990s black metal—with Burzum as

a central contributor—can be seen as a new language that radically diverged from other musical forms. The energy in the music, the idea of chaos as an ideal state, and the exploration and recognition of the dark, destructive forces within us are ideas and attitudes that are inspiring in relation to art and existence.

For the older generation of followers and music scholars, black metal is now "dead," in the sense that it no longer carries subversive power or contributes anything new as a form of expression. During the time the record store Helvete existed, run by Øystein Aarseth—the guitarist of Mayhem—black metal musicians operated under DIY principles, producing music with minimal resources for a small, dedicated audience. Today, black metal has long been commercialized, entering mainstream culture and reportedly becoming Norway's largest cultural export.

Has Norwegian black metal had a broader influence on the Norwegian art scene?
As far as we know, there is no particularly strong interest in black metal in Norwegian contemporary art. The genre can now be categorized as a somewhat niche variant of mainstream Norwegian culture and is used—either as material or reference—by artists, similar to other popular cultural expressions.

Amelia Ishmael: Bringing Black Metal into Academia

Amelia Ishmael is an artist, educator, and researcher who has taught at the School of the Art Institute of Chicago. She is perhaps one of the few scholars focusing specifically on how contemporary artists draw inspiration from black metal. Beyond her writing and research, she is also the curator of a traveling exhibition on black metal-inspired art

Interview from 2011 with Amelia Ishmael (now Amelia LiCavoli)

When did you first become interested in black metal, and when did you realize you wanted to research its influence on contemporary art? When I lived in Florida, about 14 years ago, a friend gave me a black metal mixtape. The music was unlike anything I had ever heard. It was disturbing and difficult, but at the same time it made me nervous and excited. I played that tape until it broke.

I moved to Chicago in 2009 to study art history. The music scene in Chicago is incredible. I saw bands like Locrian, Nachtmystium, Sunn O))), and also post-rock, experimental jazz, and sound artists. Switching from studio practice to studying art history was a big change, and I realized I wanted to write about how the music that artists listened to in their studios influenced and translated into their art. Many artists and designers reference heavy metal in their work, yet there was very little serious writing on the subject.

When I began talking to artists about my interest, I found that they were very curious about it. To me, it seemed like there was a real gap in scholarship. Eventually, I realized that I was most interested in how black metal affected artists—and the rest, as they say, is history.

What is the focus of your research?
When I began my research, there was very little written on the subject. I knew there was a connection between the music artists listened to and the type of work they produced, but I didn't know how to articulate it. I combined my background in art history with techniques from visual culture studies: I studied album covers and promotional images, then turned to music criticism, theory, journalism, cultural studies, documentary film, and art criticism. I spoke with artists, made studio visits, and of course, went to a lot of metal concerts.

Although black metal is an international language, my current research focuses on artists in the United States. As Brandon Stosuy pointed out in a 2009 article for the Black Metal Theory Symposium, American black metal raises many complex issues worth exploring. I've also found that my own experiences within this culture are useful reference points.

In my work I focus on a single question regarding black metal-inspired art: how a visual absence is created in artworks to make space for the music. By examining the photography, paintings, and sculptural installations of artists such as Grant Willing, Terence Hannum, and Banks Violette, I explore how sound environments are expressed in landscapes, on concert stages, and in gallery installations. If you don't recognize that black metal has its own visual language, or that sound and image are linked in these works, you can't fully grasp the intense sonic activity that occurs in this apparent void.

Black metal is often seen as a male-dominated world. What is it like being a female researcher in this field? I imagine academia isn't always open to research on a popular culture like black metal either.

That's a very interesting question—one I haven't really thought much about, which is ironic since the idea for this project actually came from a gender studies course I took with my advisor, Maud Lavin. There aren't many women involved in these discussions. Aspasia Stephanou and I spoke at the Black Metal Theory Symposium in London, and Elodie Lesourd has contributed to *C.S.* journal. I also had a female student last term who was the vocalist in a black metal band—but it's rare.

The tension between metal fans and academia is strong and won't disappear anytime soon. As someone who loves both black metal and art history, I cross boundaries between two worlds that rarely meet. I often hear art historians complain that my project leans too much toward popular culture, or they expect me to just write about black metal's music history, or they find it inappropriate that I focus on such young artists. Some metal fans complain that the artists I write about aren't "authentic" enough, or that using academic terms to describe black metal ruins the illusion of purity and rawness. I think it's important to challenge those illusions—in both camps. Always.

What characterizes black metal art?
Black metal is often seen as very formulaic. Black metal = Norway + solitude on icy mountains + black leather and spikes + corpse paint + criminal tendencies. Some artists still romanticize these clichés, but overall, that definition is pretty boring.
The artists I find most interesting are those who merge these influences with contemporary ideas to create new challenges. Choosing artists to work with has been a personal challenge, because black metal means different things to different people—which is part of the point. There's still a lot of interest in the occult, the individual, the unknown, and extreme experiences—but these are no longer strict rules. Much of my work has therefore involved developing a methodology for defining what black metal art actually is.

How do you see the future of black metal as an academic subject?
From what I've seen so far, I think my work will encourage more discussions, especially

interdisciplinary ones. I hope to help remove some of the outdated stigmas attached to black metal, and encourage those who are interested but hesitant to join the conversation.

Black Thorns in the White Cube — exhibition

Black Thorns in the White Cube was a traveling gallery exhibition curated by Amelia Ishmael that examines how contemporary artists draw visual, mythological, and emotional inspiration from black metal. The exhibition premiered in the United States in early 2012, at Paragraph Gallery in Kansas City, MO and then moving to Western Exhibitions in Chicago. The logo to the exhibition was a work by Christophe Szpajdel, known as the "lord of logos".

The Premise & Tone

Ishmael frames the exhibition with an opening meditation likening the experience of black metal art to collecting thorny vines—gloves on, trying to box them up, binding them—but always with the risk of getting scratched, the thorns piercing through. The metaphor sets up the tension that runs through the show: black metal as force, as something that resists containment, that pushes beyond boundaries.

Artists & Works

The show brings together eight artists from the U.S. and Europe, including Alexander Binder (Germany),

Vincent Como, Terence Hannum, Karlynn Holland, Elodie Lesourd, Aaron Metté, Grant Willing, Christophe Szpajdel, and Tereza Zelenkova. These creators work across media—photography, prints, drawings, artist books—and engage with black metal iconography and themes in varied, often subtle, ways.

Their artworks explore haunted Germanic forests, voids, western landscapes stripped bare, pictorial approaches to sonic experiences, and investigations into the ontology of logos (the visual branding of black metal bands). In other words, the artists don't just reference black metal; they attempt to translate its atmospheres, symbols, and mythologies into visual form.

Significance & Disruption

What makes *Black Thorns in the White Cube* important is not simply that it collects art referencing black metal, but that it participates in black metal theory: it contributes to the academic and visual discourse about how this subculture's mythology, aesthetic codes, and sonic intensity are being transformed in contemporary art. Ishmael's curation highlights how violence, obscurity, folklore, landscape, and symbol can be reimagined outside the music context—yet still carry much of its power.

Bjarne Melgaard: Sons of Odins

Bjarne Melgaard (b. 1967), a Norwegian-born artist, has intricately woven the raw intensity of black metal into his visual art, creating a compelling dialogue between music, identity, and societal critique. His collaborations with iconic black metal bands such as Mayhem, Satyricon, Darkthrone, and Thorns have not only influenced his artistic trajectory but have also positioned him as a pivotal figure in bridging the realms of extreme music and contemporary art.

Initially indifferent to black metal during his youth in Norway, Melgaard's perspective shifted upon relocating abroad. He began to perceive the genre as a contemporary manifestation of existential despair, akin to Edvard Munch's iconic painting "The Scream." Melgaard sought to channel this profound emotional resonance into his art, aiming to evoke similar visceral reactions through his work.

His artistic endeavors led to collaborations that blurred the lines between performance art and music. Notably, Melgaard partnered with Frost of Satyricon to create the performance piece "Kill Me Before I Do It Myself," (2001 – 2002) which involved aggressive acts of destruction and blasphemy, challenging audiences to confront themes of violence and nihilism.

Visually, Melgaard's works often incorporate elements reminiscent of black metal aesthetics—dark, chaotic, and emotionally charged. His paintings, such as the

2015 "Untitled," utilize oil on canvas combined with mixed media elements like synthetic hair and makeup products, creating textured surfaces that invite tactile engagement. These pieces resonate with the anarchic spirit of black metal, reflecting themes of alienation and societal critique.

In essence, Bjarne Melgaard's art serves as a conduit for exploring the profound emotional landscapes of black metal. Through his collaborations and artworks, he has not only redefined the boundaries of contemporary art but has also highlighted the enduring relevance of black metal as a medium for expressing complex themes of identity, rebellion, and existential angst.

Sons of Odin

When Bjarne Melgaard returned to Stockholm with the exhibition *Sons of Odin* (2011) at Galleri Lars Bohman, the controversy that had surrounded his earlier works seemed to have subsided. Known for provocative pieces like the video *All Gym Queens Deserve to Die* and the scandal over his *Mader* photographs at the Historiska Museet, Melgaard now turned his attention to the world of Norwegian black metal—and in particular, to the band Mayhem.

The installation opened with photographs of burning churches, iconic images tied to the mythology of black metal's second wave. These photographs formed part of a larger work titled *Dead and Euronymous in*

Heaven, which combined documentary-style images with a staged environment: a cage, a sofa, an altar-like table with figurines, and even a bonsai tree from which a bound figure was suspended. The atmosphere was deliberately restrained, as though Melgaard sought to give chaotic material a paradoxical clarity through order.

The exhibition also included paintings rendered in trembling strokes reminiscent of Edvard Munch. Layers of overlapping figures suggested fractured moments of time, dissolving the boundaries between truth and fiction, morality and fantasy. The familiar symbols of the black metal world—blood, weapons, corpse paint, inverted figures—appeared like fragments in a fever dream.

Unlike some of his earlier work, *Sons of Odin* featured fewer textual elements. Words were often crossed out, overwritten, or rendered meaningless through paradoxical statements—an echo of Melgaard's ongoing interest in undermining language itself.

Through these works, Melgaard treated black metal not as pure shock value but as a cultural fiction—a mythology steeped in violence, chaos, and transgression. By reframing Mayhem's notorious history within the structures of contemporary art, he both exposed and reimagined the aesthetics of extremity, capturing the uneasy tension between destruction and form.

Peter Beste and Torbjørn Rødland: Photography and Black Metal

From the start, photography has been central to the myth of black metal. The genre's corpse-painted faces, ruined churches, and stark landscapes are inseparable from the sound itself, and a number of photographers have sought to capture that world with their own artistic language. Among them, two stand out: Peter Beste and Torbjørn Rødland, who in very different ways documented and reimagined the black metal scene.

Peter Beste (b. 1978, USA) is best known for his monumental project True Norwegian Black Metal (2008), the result of eight years of immersion in Norway's underground. His portraits of figures like Gaahl, Abbath, and Infernus combine gritty realism with a sense of theatrical staging. Beste's lens reveals the contradictions of the scene: fierce corpse-painted musicians in remote forests, but also mundane glimpses of everyday life. The images have become iconic, shaping how an international audience visualizes the genre.

Torbjørn Rødland (b. 1970, Norway) approaches photography differently. Known for his surreal, unsettling images that blur beauty and discomfort, Rødland engaged directly with black metal in his early-2000s series Black. In this work, he photographed musicians in full corpse paint, not on stage but in natural environments—Norwegian forests heavy with symbolism. For Rødland, the forest was a stronger backdrop than any urban setting, a space where ritual, nostalgia, and performance fused. In Black, the collaboration between photographer and musicians reflects a shared desire to intensify reality, to make the image as charged as the music itself.

Together, Beste and Rødland reveal two poles of black metal photography. Beste acts as the ethnographer, embedding himself in the subculture and portraying its raw life from within. Rødland transforms its aesthetics into art photography, situating black metal imagery within broader conversations about myth, nature, and the uncanny. Their work shows how the visual dimension of black metal is not secondary to the music, but a parallel art form that continues to shape the genre's legacy.

Maddie Leach: *The Grief Prophesy*

Maddie Leach is a visual artist from Sweden whose work in the 2010s turned directly toward questions of memory, identity, and subcultural myth — in particular, the Swedish black metal scene of the 1990s. Her project *The Grief Prophesy*, shown in *GIBCA 2017*, uses the history of Dissection (one of Sweden's most influential black metal bands) as a lens through which to explore symbolism, violence, hidden histories, and the politics of belonging.

Her work draws both on local Swedish culture and on the international imagery of black metal — its symbols, its myth-making, its burdens. But rather than romanticising or simply documenting, Leach re-frames those symbols (pentagrams, inverted crosses, occult iconography) in relation to violence (both personal and social), intersectionality, and changing urban society (for example, migration and diversity in Göteborg).

The Grief Prophesy refers in its title to Dissection's first demo (*The Grief Prophecy*, 1991). But Leach doesn't merely re-play old ideas: she reenvisions holding space for what was erased, hidden, or silenced. She works with Kristian Wåhlin (aka Necrolord), who originally designed many Dissection album covers, asking him to create an image of Keillers Park and its water tower in Göteborg — the site connected to the hate murder of Josef Ben Meddour in 1997. The juxtaposition is powerful: the satanic symbols and subcultural imagery of Dissection's folklore; the real human violence with its prejudice; and the evolving city whose demographics and sensibilities have shifted.

She also created a new vinyl release that reinterprets Dissection's *Into Infinity Obscurity* in a slow instrumental way, using instruments like the vevlira (a traditional Swedish folk instrument) and oud (from North Africa / Middle East). The auditory component becomes a lament, matching the visual and symbolic work: mourning what was lost, what has been hidden, what must be remembered.

Leach's proposal to carve a right-side-up pentagram at the site of the inverted one, as a memorial for Josef Ben Meddour, is an act of symbolic resistance — turning meaning, reclaiming space — though it was not permitted. Still, the attempt itself is meaningful, as part of the project's insistence that symbols and spaces matter.

Banks Violette: Black Metal Church

Banks Violette (b. 1973) is an American artist whose work translates the iconography and mythologies of subcultural violence into the register of contemporary sculpture and installation. Using glossy black surfaces, cast salt, fluorescent fixtures, charred forms, and sound, Violette builds austere tableaux that resemble stage sets for loss and ruin. Rather than documenting black metal directly, his practice extracts the movement's symbolic grammar — burned churches, ruined altars, ritual theatre — and restages it as a conceptual inquiry into belief, spectacle, and the aesthetics of extremity.

A pivotal moment in Violette's engagement with black metal occurred with his 2005 commission at the Whitney Museum of American Art in New York City (2005). For this exhibition, Violette erected a life-sized reconstruction of a burned-out church on a black stage, inspired by an image from a black metal album cover. Surrounding the installation was a 5.1 surround sound score composed by Thorns Ltd (Snorre Ruch), a Norwegian black metal musician whose history is intertwined with some of the scene's most infamous acts of violence, including church arsons and the 1993 murder of Øystein Aarseth (Euronymous), guitarist of Mayhem, by Varg Vikernes. According to Violette, the work was inspired by these instances of extremity within the scene, translating both real and symbolic acts of destruction into a conceptual framework. By reconstituting the ruin as a pristine, uncanny object accompanied by Ruch's ambiences, Violette forced viewers to confront the tension between aestheticized devastation and historical violence. Critics noted how the piece mediated between documentary horror and minimalist spectacle, asking whether belief and myth can be separated from their destructive consequences.

Violette's broader practice continues to explore the intersection of black metal aesthetics and conceptual art. He frequently references the iconography of ruin, decay, and ritual that permeates the music: skeletal stage sets, blackened altars, and abandoned structures become sculptural objects that evoke both the theatricality and extremity of the subculture. Works like his salt-encrusted stage installations or collapsed chandelier pieces turn motifs of destruction into objects of reflection, forcing the viewer to negotiate the tension between fascination and repulsion.

His engagement with black metal is less about fandom and more about the symbolic power of the scene. Bands such as Mayhem, Burzum, and Thorns Ltd provide both inspiration and historical context; their stories of violence, ritual, and myth-making become a lens through which Violette examines belief, ideology, and the aesthetics of extremity. In his work, destruction and monumentality coexist: ruined forms are carefully composed, creating a paradoxical elegance that mirrors the tension between black metal's anti-commercial ethos and its aesthetic potency.

In this way, Banks Violette's work exemplifies the dialogue between subculture and gallery, showing how black metal's visual and symbolic power can be reinterpreted, abstracted, and elevated into contemporary art. The same intensity that animates the music — fascination with ruin, extremity, and ritual — is transformed in his work into a conceptual exploration of the dark aesthetics of belief and spectacle, a space where the mythic and the historical collide.

Élodie Lesourd: Deconstructing Black Metal

Élodie Lesourd (b. 1978, France) is a contemporary artist and curator whose work explores the visual and philosophical dimensions of black metal. Across her practice, Lesourd investigates the aesthetics of darkness, ritual, and extremity, translating the imagery and mythologies of the scene into a conceptual language that belongs as much to contemporary art as to music subculture.

In the 2017 exhibition *Black Thorns in the White Cube*, curated by Amelia Ishmael, Lesourd presented a series of works that deconstruct the logos of seminal Norwegian black metal bands. By extending and connecting the sharp extremities of these logos, she revealed hidden geometries and abstracted forms, turning symbols of aggression and secrecy into minimal, almost architectural compositions. Through this approach, Lesourd both critiques and reframes black metal iconography, inviting viewers to reconsider the semiotic power and aesthetic allure of these extreme cultural markers.

Another significant work, *Pictures of You (As Dead as Euronymous)*, engages directly with black metal history. The piece references Øystein "Euronymous" Aarseth, the guitarist of Mayhem, whose murder in 1993 by Varg Vikernes remains one of the most notorious events in the scene. Lesourd's work neither sensationalizes nor memorializes the act; instead, it interrogates how black metal's tragedies have been mythologized and consumed as part of its visual and cultural narrative.

Her *Inner (Black Metal)* (2008), a polyurethane painting on steel, embodies the dark, skeletal qualities of black metal in a more abstract form. Stark, minimal, and meditative, the work reflects the genre's preoccupations with death, decay, and existential intensity, translating them into a visual vocabulary that feels both immediate and metaphysical.

Lesourd's engagement with black metal is not limited to her own studio practice. As a curator, she has explored the dialogue between the music and contemporary visual art in exhibitions such as *FREUX FOLLETS* (2015), co-curated with Erik Smith. These projects bring together artists whose work resonates with the symbolism, ritual, and extremity of black metal, situating the genre within a broader artistic and cultural discourse.

Writing has also been a vital component of her practice. In her essay *Baptism or Death*, Lesourd reflects on black metal as more than music: a philosophical and aesthetic system that challenges conventional notions of beauty, aligning more closely with the Baroque's embrace of chaos and excess. She proposes that black metal functions as a Gesamtkunstwerk—a total work of art—where sound, imagery, and ideology intertwine, producing a sensibility that contemporary art can engage, analyze, and translate.

Through her work as both artist and curator, Élodie Lesourd situates black metal within the conceptual and visual frameworks of contemporary art, transforming the extremity of the scene into forms of reflection, abstraction, and critical dialogue. Her practice illuminates how a subculture rooted in darkness and transgression can speak to broader questions of myth, ritual, and the aesthetics of extremity.

Summary

Black metal, once a rebellious subculture defined by its raw sound, anti-establishment ethos, and provocative imagery, has undergone a significant transformation. Emerging from the underground music scene, it has found a place within the hallowed walls of the white cube, the epitome of institutionalized art spaces. This journey reflects broader cultural shifts and the evolving relationship between subcultures and the art world.

Theoretical Foundations: Subculture and Art

In the book *Subculture: The Meaning of Style* (1979), Dick Hebdige argues that postwar British youth subcultures, such as punks and skinheads, use distinctive styles in clothing, music, and mannerisms as a symbolic form of resistance against the dominant ideology and hegemony of mainstream society. Hebdige applies semiotic analysis, treating subcultural styles as "texts," to show how these styles disrupt the established system of meaning and represent a temporary blockage to normalization. However, he also explains that these once-subversive symbols are often commodifiied by capitalism and re-appropriated by the dominant culture, ultimately losing their rebellious power and becoming integrated into the mainstream

Black metal, with its corpse paint, inverted crosses, forest imagery, and preoccupation with night and decay, originally embodied a form of cultural resistance. It created a symbolic universe that opposed mainstream values, giving voice to marginalized perspectives and alternative ways of thinking. Yet, over time, this once-radical subculture has been partially absorbed by the mainstream and commodified, its symbols and aesthetics circulating in broader cultural and commercial contexts.

Building on Hebdige, scholars such as Sarah Thornton (*Club Cultures*, 1995) and Andy Bennett have discussed how subcultural forms mediate social identity and collective experience. Black metal, in this sense, functions not merely as a musical genre but as a broader cultural system—its aesthetic choices, performance practices, and mythologies contributing to a shared sense of existential confrontation with modern life.

Existentialism and Contemporary Society

Central to black metal is a preoccupation with existential themes: death, impermanence, solitude, and the absurdity of existence. In contemporary society—marked by technological acceleration, climate anxiety, political instability, and social alienation—these themes resonate powerfully. Black metal confronts the realities that many find overwhelming, offering a symbolic space to explore despair, nihilism, and transcendence.

Artists translating these ideas into visual art create work that channels a similar confrontation with the human condition. In sculpture, painting, and installation, the darkness of black metal becomes a tool for reflection: it externalizes internal anxieties, the invisible pressures of contemporary life, and the awareness of mortality. This existential engagement aligns with the function of art across history, where encounters with death, decay, and the sublime have long served as catalysts for reflection and aesthetic experience.

Connections to Art History

Black metal's thematic focus on darkness and mortality finds parallels in several historical periods of artistic preoccupation with death and the sublime. The Romantic era, with painters such as Caspar David Friedrich, Johan Christian Dahl, and Marcus Larson, explored fog-draped landscapes, ruined abbeys, and solitary figures dwarfed by nature, visually embodying melancholy, awe, and existential contemplation. Similarly, Symbolist artists such as Edvard Munch or Odilon Redon delved into psychic landscapes, mortality, and psychological extremes, echoing black metal's fascination with inner darkness.

Later periods, including Expressionism and Surrealism, continued to confront inner turmoil, societal anxieties, and mortality, often employing abstraction and distortion. Black metal shares this concern, translating fear, alienation, and obsession with death into sound and visual motifs. Contemporary artists such as Banks Violette, Élodie Lesourd, and Maddie Leach adopt similar strategies—using ruins, abstraction, ritual imagery, and skeletal forms—to bridge the gap between black metal's subcultural iconography and broader aesthetic inquiry.

The Journey from Subculture to White Cube

The path of black metal from subculture to white cube has been gradual but decisive. Initially dismissed as extreme or irrelevant, its aesthetic and philosophical depth began attracting the attention of contemporary artists and curators. By recontextualizing black metal imagery within art galleries and museums, artists like Banks Violette and Lesourd force a critical reflection on violence, ritual, mortality, and the allure of darkness.

This transformation also highlights the enduring relevance of subcultures as sources of artistic inspiration. Norwegian black metal, in particular, has become emblematic because of its extreme fidelity to thematic and visual codes, its historical narratives of transgression, and its mythicized connection to landscape and folklore. Its combination of sonic intensity, symbolic richness, and existential gravitas makes it particularly fertile for contemporary artistic exploration.

Conclusion

Black metal's journey from underground subculture to contemporary art exemplifies the dialogue between societal anxieties, aesthetic expression, and historical consciousness. Its existential themes resonate with contemporary society's struggles with impermanence, alienation, and fear, while its visual language echoes centuries of artistic engagement with death, darkness, and the sublime. In the hands of artists translating these motifs into sculpture, painting, and installation, black metal emerges as a conceptual tool, a bridge between subcultural extremity and the reflective spaces of the white cube, demonstrating the enduring power of darkness to inspire both cultural critique and aesthetic innovation.

www.ingramcontent.com/pod-product-compliance
Lightning Source LLC
Chambersburg PA
CBHW050017230526
45470CB00003B/1005